Practical Wisdom for
Leaders in Recreation

Advance Praise for
Lead With Your HEART

"I wish that I had Edith's book at the beginning of my career. Absorb it, use it and apply it and you will be a great leader. It is an easy read with lots of examples and Edith outlines actions for leaders to take. Most of us learn by example and it is easy to pick out the bad examples. Edith provides the tools. So get out there, put your HEART in it and be a good example!"

—Ron Kirstein
Former Recreation Educator, Camosun College,
British Columbia

"A useful easy-to-read and interesting book that is very applicable to the recreation industry. The mix of information, tips and anecdotal information will keep you interested and inspire you to reflect on your personal leadership."

—Erin Pickard
Recreation Coordinator, St. Albert, Alberta

"Edith provides a simple and practical guide anyone can relate to. She has always been a great HEART leader who is willing to share her expertise and experience."

—Barb Costache,
CAO, Alberta Life Saving Society, Edmonton

"Having worked with Edith in a volunteer setting and with Edith and her team professionally, I can assure you that this book captures the very essence of what makes Edith such a wonderful leader. An easy read and full of useful practical ideas to help make you the Leader you want to be."

—Loie Unwin
Certified Executive Coach, www.drumawillan.com

"I can say with certainty that Edith demonstrated leadership with HEART when she was my manager. There is something to be said about walking the talk. "Edith shares her practiced leadership advice in an easy-to-read and reflective format."

—Liette Jorgensen
Recreation Team Member

"An enjoyable read on key aspects for training, corporate culture and leadership. The HEART concept provides a guideline for supervisors in many industries to do things right-the first time."

—Gerhard Weiss
CEO, WAPOTEC, water and air systems

LEAD WITH YOUR HEART

Developing and Leading Teams that Care

EDITH MARTIN

The Rec Coach's™
Lead with Your HEART
Developing and Leading Teams that Care
Edith Martin

Library and Archives Canada Cataloguing in Publications
ISBN-13: 978-1497383227
ISBN-10: 1497383226
TheRecCoach.com

Cover design by: Ares Jun

Photo by:
Jeff Hopper, UP photographics

Dedication

As I wrote this book, my mother, Ruth, age 93,
continued to be a source of support. I am grateful
for the love and encouragement my parents have
given me throughout my life.

John and Ruth Jackson
This book is dedicated to them.

Acknowledgments

I have really appreciated the assistance of my writing coach and developmental editor, Kathrin Lake, for her guidance and inspiration helping me create this book from start to finish.

I owe a great deal to the hundreds of staff I have had the privilege of leading and to those who led me. It is from them that I learned and practiced my skills in leadership, teamwork and customer service.

Thank you to the following individuals for their time and energy providing feedback:

Bill Holtby, Ron Kirstein, Bill Metcalfe, Jerry Spencer, Gerhard Weiss, Erin Pickard, Barb Costache, Loie Unwin, Liette Jorgensen, Stephania Duffee, Ross Tyson, John Younie, Darel Baker, Holly Pickle, Brian Sullivan, Pat Church, Gaylien Larita, Ellen Chauvet, Linda Robertson, Robin and Gerda Francis, Lee Garstang, Sharon Cox and Carol Jackson.

I have many friends and family members who also shared their encouragement in this process especially my husband and best friend Darrel, who is always there for me.

Contents

Introduction 1

Chapter 1
HELP 5
employees have a good start with clear expectations

Chapter 2
ENCOURAGE.. 17
team members to make connections and support
one another

Chapter 3
ACKNOWLEDGE 31
feedback and why work is important

Chapter 4
ROLE MODEL.. 47
the right things and learn how paying attention
pays off

Chapter 5
TRUST... 65
your team members and gain their trust

The Rec Coach's suggested Reading List. 85

About the Author 89

INTRODUCTION

"Lead with your heart
and
your team will never let you down!"
Edith Martin, The Rec Coach

I was born to teach. Leadership started at age five. My neighborhood friends and little sister were my students. My classroom was set up in a square hallway on the lower floor of our split-level house. My pupils sat in little desks made by my father. A small blackboard hung on the wall at the perfect height. I always felt confident in this space. I was doing what I loved to do; helping others learn.

However when I think back to my first supervisory position, I wished I had had a teacher then. There were many times I could have used a mentor to teach me some quick tips and techniques so my staff didn't get the brunt of my trial and errors. Thank goodness for the wisdom I came to rely on from the pages of the many leadership books I read.

I am very grateful for many authors, especially Ken Blanchard, author of *The One Minute Manager*. His writing had a real impact on my leadership development and has inspired the writing of these books. Later, institutional training in Education and Human Resources continued my learning journey.

Over the years, I have worked for and have been influenced by many different leaders. I have learned many valuable lessons that I know will be helpful for both new and experienced supervisors, and now I am doing what I feel I was meant to do - teach it!

The Rec Coach series includes real life stories with practical tips and suggestions for effective leadership, teamwork and customer service. The names and personal characteristics of the individuals in the stories have been changed in order to disguise identities.

This book, *Lead with Your Heart* is the first in my series on leadership directed toward recreation facility managers and supervisors. It can be of value for any leaders in any occupation. This book shares my five leadership keys and the importance of a leadership style that encompasses my values:

Help .... team members get a good start

Encourage .... team members to support one another

Acknowledge ..... feedback and why work is important

Role model .... the right things to develop leaders

Trust .... team members and the team

At the beginning of each chapter is a head's up that focuses on the points I will be making. At the end of each story I have recapped my best advice, included questions for you to reflect on, and to consider how to take action in your own situation. At the back of the book are blank note pages for planning the leadership action you want to take.

Chapter One

HELP

*"A good objective of leadership is to **help** those who are doing poorly to do well and to **help** those who are doing well to do even better."*
—Jim Rohn, Author and Motivational Speaker

The Rec Coach's Heads up on HELP
HELP team members have a great start.
HELP them understand what is expected of them.

First Day on the Job!

On a wet spring day, I wanted to arrive early for my new summer position. I was excited to have full time work as a field consultant. As I climbed two flights of stairs to the office, I felt anxious not knowing what was in store for me. Approaching the reception area, the lady sitting behind the desk looked over her glasses and greeted me.

"Good morning. How can I help you?"

"My name is Edith. I am the new field consultant. This is my first day. Tom is my supervisor."

"Well, I'm Joan, it is nice to meet you. Tom's not in yet. Why don't you take a seat over here for now?"

"Thanks"

My work was to start at 9 a.m. and Tom arrived at 9:20 a.m. When he came in, he looked surprised and said,

"Oh, I forgot you were starting today. Please come with me. I'll show you where your desk will be."

As I sat down at my workstation, Tom proceeded to pull each drawer out and show me the stationary supplies available for me to use, ones obviously left from the previous employee. He indicated that four other staff members share the same office although at the time, I could only see one other person at the desk in the corner by the window.

"Meet Claire, she looks after the coordination of all the program materials."

Claire looked up from her work.

"Hi, you must be the new person that was just hired? I'm here if you need any help."

"Thanks. I'm Edith. Nice to meet you. I'm sure I will be asking lots of questions."

"No problem, anytime" Claire indicated. Tom piped up, now in a rush.

"Well, I am off to a meeting and won't be back until sometime this afternoon."

I responded, "Thank you. See you later," but my mind was racing with questions. *Wow, was that it? Was that my orientation?*

As it turned out, it was up to me to determine where to start, which direction I would go in and to figure out what was expected of me in this position.

It took weeks to really feel comfortable and know that I was on the right track.

Now I compare this to organizations that gave me a great start. They believed orientation was important. They had a plan, were well prepared and provided a great introduction. They also believed in a continuous learning environment.

"Help Ensure a Great Start"

Keep in mind that an effective orientation gives the new employee a great introduction, helps them to feel welcome and also an important part of the team.

An effective orientation helps them to understand their specific role, connect personally to the organization's mission and learn how their work ultimately makes a difference.

- **Make a detailed checklist** of the important key aspects you want the new employee to learn initially about the organization and about their position.

- **Plan a schedule** including blocks of time when the new employee will meet with others to get a good understanding of who does what and how they work together.

- **Assign a buddy** or a mentor so the new employee has a go to colleague for questions and assistance. Make sure the buddy and/or mentor knows what is expected in this assigned role.

- **Allow enough time** for the orientation to occur over several days and weeks so the new employee has time to review materials, ask questions, to meet and learn from others on the team.
- **Provide continuous support.** A front line employee should never be left to fend for him or herself until completing their orientation and feeling comfortable with their role.
- **Plan for follow up** and to check in with the new employee.

Take Action!
What will you do to help ensure team members have a great start?
- How will you prepare for a new member's arrival to make them feel welcome?
- How will you make their first day, first week and first month of work special and memorable?
- What is the plan for their orientation and who is involved in ensuring a great start?
- When will you schedule times for checking in and following up with the new member?

Story 2 - HELP

Caught off Guard!

Everyone has experienced situations when you didn't know what to expect and been caught off guard, felt unprepared, inadequate or really "dumb" because you just didn't know. When you start off in a new job, nobody wants to experience this. I recall some advice I recently learned from a six year old. When asked a question that she couldn't answer, she simply replied:

"I don't know, I haven't learned that yet".

I remember a time when I was really caught off guard. I was 20 and had applied for a manager's position for a summer job at an outdoor swimming pool. I was called for an interview and told to meet at a certain time in the town office boardroom. When I arrived to see eight people sitting around the table, including Town Councilors and Recreation

Board Members, you can imagine how intimidated I was.

My previous job interviews involved having a short discussion with the Recreation Director and having been hired on the spot. This time was obviously different! They asked me to sit at the head of the table. Each person took turns asking me a question. Talk about a situation that puts you on your toes and having to think fast on your feet. I did my best and was the successful candidate. I am sure it wouldn't have had anything to do with the fact that my uncle was Mayor of the town at the time. Back then I didn't realize that this experience would give me a real advantage for all other interviews I would ever have in the future.

It was in this position that I also experienced a situation that challenged my expectations. The records from the previous years had been thrown away. There was nothing to show what had been done in the past, no programs, no facility or staff schedules or maintenance information to reference. I had to start from scratch.

I spent the entire summer creating documents that would provide guidance and examples for the next supervisor to follow. I didn't want anyone else to go through this experience. I tried to develop everything to help make expectations clear for future staff. I had no idea that what I created would have a lasting impact. Years later I ran into a colleague who had worked in the same position. He asked if I was the Edith who created the facility operation manuals that were so helpful.

Think about the times you have started a new position and the expectations of you were not clear. The anxiety and stress of your first year in any job is hard enough even if you are fortunate to have a good orientation to the position.

When expectations are not clear:
- Employees don't know what they are supposed to do.
- They don't know why they should do something.
- They don't know what is important.
- They are put in a situation that makes them feel inadequate!

It is really obvious when staff are not well trained. I strongly believe that this is one of the main reasons why organizations experience so much turnover of part time and casual staff.

"Help Ensure Expectations are Clear"

- **Show and tell what is expected.** The position description is a good start but it usually doesn't cover everything.
- **Ensure they have reference materials** to find answers especially for frequently asked questions.
- **Have a communication system** for employees to keep up-to-date with the changes that occur between each shift. Provide continuous updates on what is new, what has changed.
  (Could use a message book, emails, tweets, newsletters, posts, blogs, Facebook, Twitter, tail gate meetings, team huddle at the start of each shift etc.)
- **Ensure team members are knowledgeable** about the facility, the programs and the services offered and where they can access resource information.

- **<u>Allow employees to experience or participate</u>** in activities so they are better informed and able to answer any questions customers may have.
- **<u>Encourage team members to ask a million questions</u>** until expectations are really clear.

Take Action!
What will you do to help ensure expectations are clear?
- How will you ensure that the staff understand what is expected of them?
- What systems will you have for communicating effectively?
- What is the plan for regular follow up and guidance in the future?
- What additional training needs to be planned for them?

Chapter Two

ENCOURAGE

"What people want is a feeling of importance, a feeling of impact, a feeling of influence"
—Ray Stata, Co-founder & Chairman
of Analogue Devices

The Rec Coach's Heads Up on Encourage:
ENCOURAGE team members to make connections.
ENCOURAGE them to support one another.

Story 1 - ENCOURAGE

Connect and Communicate!

Gaby was one of our feisty seniors. She was tall, thin with fiery red hair and a chronic complainer. She used the facility several times a week, arriving all set to go in her bathing suit and cover up, with her bathing cap, mask and snorkel already on. When it rained, we would see her coming down the walkway in a bright blue raincoat and rubber boots.

For many years she complained about something nearly every day she was there and many of her concerns were petty:

"The pool is too crowded"

"The showers are too hot (or too cold) and the spray is too forceful."

"The mirrors in the locker room are in the wrong place"

"There should be a clock on every wall"

The customer service representatives always respectfully listened to her concerns and passed them on to a shift supervisor. They would follow up and do their best to deal with each situation, often taking the approach of asking for Gaby's suggestions in resolving some of the issues. She never had much of a response although Gaby was always encouraged to provide her feedback at any time.

It seemed there was no satisfying our chronic complainers and the team felt that people like this have a special mission in their lives; their mission to complain, push people's buttons and forever test our patience.

Chronic complainers are like children who misbehave. They both crave attention. The best way to deal with a 'Gaby' was to make a connection by getting to know the things in Gaby's life that were important to her.

Team members were encouraged to strike up a conversation by asking any number of questions such as:

How long have you lived in the city?
What do you like to do in the community?
What is a favorite past time?

After team members had conversations with Gaby, the picture became clear. She had lived in the community for more than 30 years and had not been actively involved lately because of spending most of her time taking care of her ill husband. When he passed away, Gaby was very lonely. She came to the facility because it made her feel better.

Conversations help make connections. Connections help build relationships and provide an opportunity to demonstrate that you care.

After taking the time to get to know Gaby, we noticed that the chronic complaining eventually subsided. Her focus had changed. She often brought the staff interesting articles and books to read. She had quality conversations with team members who were able to listen, learn and show they cared.

Another senior patron, Bob, a short, timid gentleman in his late seventies was a chronic rule breaker. Bob never said too much and didn't like to make eye contact. He would insist on bringing his safety razor with him out on the pool deck and use it in the steam room and sauna.

The lifeguards approached him several times to let him know that this behavior was inappropriate and disrespectful of the other patrons. Yet, on many occasions he had to be reminded, and the supervisor on duty spoke to him as well. Bob even tried to be sneaky, hiding his razor in the side of his swimsuit.

Why was Bob acting like a little kid? He was certainly old enough to know better. Not having any luck with Bob's lack of cooperation, the supervisor finally brought it to my attention. Again, I encouraged the team members to spend time getting to know him.

"What do you know about Bob? Have you ever had a conversation with him? Think about the many questions you can ask to get to know Bob well."

The staff decided to give it a try and went out of their way to be extra friendly. Bob used the facility on a regular basis so it didn't take long for them to find out that he also lived alone and always looked forward to coming to the facility. His wife had passed away, his children lived in other cities, he didn't have any pets and he didn't know any of his neighbors. He loved to draw and listen to the radio.

Just like Gaby, amazingly, his inappropriate behavior stopped as soon as the staff paid more attention to him and he realized how much we cared. Spending time getting to know your patrons, be they seniors, juniors or in between, will not only make their day, it will make your day more fun.

 **Advice**

"Encourage Making Connections"

The patrons who seem chronically annoying can help us learn how to make better connections, practice our conversation and listening skills, to use more compassion and therefore give us an opportunity to show that we really care.

- **<u>Encourage team members to smile,</u>** make eye contact and be friendly.
- **<u>Encourage team members to ask questions and have a dialogue.</u>** Suggest starting with general questions and then when appropriate moving to more personal questions.
  - o How did your exercise session go today?
  - o What do you like best about our facility?
  - o What could we do to help make your experience here better?
  - o Did you hear about the new program we are offering in the spring?
  - o Where were you born and raised?
  - o Would you tell me about your work career?

- **Encourage team members to ask; "How can I help"** or "Is there anything else I can do for you?"
- **Encourage keeping the conversations upbeat** and positive.

Take Action!

What will you do to encourage team members to make connections?

- How will they build positive relationships with customers?
- How will they learn about customer needs and the root of their problems?
- How will they problem solve and look for solutions?

Story 2 - ENCOURAGE

Listen Up!

16-year-old Melanie, one of the team's new customer service representatives, was trying her best to listen to a lady at the facility reception desk. The lady was complaining about her child's instructor and going on and on about how much time her daughter spends waiting for her turn to swim because the instructor insists on having each child swim one at a time. Melanie had learned that it was important to make eye contact to demonstrate that you are listening when the customer speaks so she stared at the lady's eyes continuously.

She stood patiently waiting for the lady to finish ranting and then all of a sudden the lady made two fists, slammed them down on the counter and yelled,

"Are you listening to me?"

Surprised and shocked by what this lady had just done, she blurted

"Yes of course," while at the same time could not understand why the lady reacted the way she did.

Melanie's experienced co-worker, Jane, who had been on the team for five years, was standing by. She assisted with the situation, was able to calm the lady down and discuss solutions to resolve her concerns. After the lady was on her way, Jane offered to share a teachable moment with Melanie.

Melanie asked, "Do you know why that lady was so upset with me?"

Jane explained, "The lady's perception could be that you weren't really listening. I didn't get a chance to see your facial expressions, but one possibility would be that the lady misread your body language."

Melanie felt relieved that Jane had been there to help in this situation. She had never experienced anything like this before. She appreciated Jane's support and her willingness to help. Her advice in the past was always very practical and helped build her confidence when dealing with difficult customers.

"Did you know that listening to the customer includes more than just good eye contact?"

"What do you mean? I was really trying to listen to what she was saying."

Jane smiled and said, "What I like to remember, is that I have to really *want* to listen if I want to learn." She continued to explain that the greatest respect we can give to another person is to give them our undivided attention.

"It shows that we consider them to be an important human being. Active listening means showing that you are interested, that you are actually listening and your responses focus on the person speaking".

This time, Melanie paid close attention to what Jane was saying as she continued.

"These days, people often experience neglect when being served because the customer service representative is distracted, only half listening or thinking about something else."

"That would be rude," Melanie commented.

"Besides making eye contact you can shift your posture to lean toward the person, make the occasional nod, say *uh-huh* or *I see*. Be sure to choose what feels right in the moment. To show your understanding, ask a question that follows what they have been talking about, or paraphrase what has been said."

"But the lady was so upset with me and it is hard to think of all those things when someone is ranting."

"Just take it one step at a time and be conscious of your body language. Practice with every customer you come in contact with and soon it will become automatic for you."

"Okay, I will give that a try. I guess I wasn't *really* listening"

"A couple of additional pointers Melanie. It is very important to thank the customer for bringing her concern to your attention. Once you know the details, it is good to offer options for next steps. That might be arranging for the programmer to speak to her immediately if she is available or to have the programmer contact the lady as soon as possible."

"Lastly, be sure to mention that we always appreciate getting feedback as it provides an opportunity for us to make improvements."

"Thanks for the tips Jane, I will give these new techniques a try."

Jane really was a great resource on practicing active listening, but more importantly, both of these employees supported one another. Not only was Jane supporting Melanie in a teachable moment, she gave her feedback gently and respectfully. Likewise, Melanie was not defensive that a non-manager was teaching her something. She took the support for what it was and learned from the experience. This is how staff are able to support one another, and lead one another.

 **Advice**

"Encourage Staff to Support One Another"

Sharing ideas with open minds is crucial for teamwork and building relationships. All team members should be encouraged to share any ideas and opinions they have. This helps team members feel important and have an opportunity to influence.

- **Encourage new team members to ask questions** and share their ideas to make change.
- **Set up a system** for new team members to work and learn from experienced team members.
- **Encourage paying attention** to how each other deals with situations.
- **Role model** and encourage good listening.
- **Encourage debriefing sessions** especially after experiencing a stressful and or challenging situation.
- **Provide training** on how to give and receive feedback effectively.
- **Encourage giving feedback**- on each others work performance.

Take Action!
How will you encourage an environment of supporting one another?

- What are you doing to encourage good listening?
- What are you doing to encourage team members supporting one another?
- What are you doing to encourage effective giving and receiving feedback?
- What are you doing to encourage the sharing of everyone's ideas and opinions?

Chapter Three

ACKNOWLEDGE

*"Real life isn't always going to be perfect or go our way, but that recurring **acknowledgement** of what is working in our lives can help us not only survive but surmount our difficulties"*

—Sarah Ban Breathnach, author of
Simple Abundance

The Rec Coach's Heads Up on Acknowledge:
ACKNOWLEDGE team member's feedback.
ACKNOWLEDGE why their work is important.

Story 1 - ACKNOWLEDGE

The Truth Can Hurt!

At one point in my career, I was asked to provide assistance in another department for almost a year. When I returned to my regular position, I didn't get off to a very good start. As a leader I went through a period of time when I only saw what was not going well.

Barry, one of my confident, young staff members who worked on a part-time basis while attending university, contacted me to set a time to meet. I was thinking and hoping that he wasn't going to tell me that he needed to resign because of his studies. Barry was a stellar employee; very responsible with a superb work ethic, always taking the initiative to ensure things got done.

When he came into my office he said, "Thanks for taking the time to meet with me. I have a question for you and I hope that you will take it the right way."

After a long pause he asked, "Where did the positive leader go that we once had?" He continued by explaining, "You have always been encouraging and inspiring, but since you came back you have not been the same".

At that moment a number of questions went through my head. *How could I have turned so negative? How many others on the team were feeling the same way? What caused me to be so negative and what had I done since coming back to my position? How did Barry have the courage to bring this to my attention?*

I felt so terrible that I had let my team down. I felt ashamed that I hadn't treated them very well since my return. No one wants to work in an environment with a negative leader!

"I am so grateful that you have had the courage to share your thoughts with me Barry. I feel so bad that I have let you and the rest of the team down."

With a tear in my eye and a lump in my throat I said, "You know it is up to me to change all this. Thank you so much for letting me know."

Taking a minute for this to sink in, I asked him a parting question.

"Would you help me by providing further feedback in a week or so?" He smiled.

"Yes, of course, I would be happy to help".

I had always read that change starts with you, and you need to be the change that you want to see in the world. Change can happen immediately. All you have to do is to decide to do things differently. This can be done in an instant!

After a sleepless night thinking about all the negative comments I would have made in the past couple of weeks, I decided to come up with a plan to change from that day forward. My plan included the acknowledgement of the mistakes I had made to my team members and to never use a "finding the negative" approach again. It obviously did nothing to inspire or encourage others.

It took courage but I admitted that

"I hadn't been a very good role model and my approach to communication had been very negative."

I also shared how grateful I was that Barry had the courage to bring this to my attention. I hoped everyone would forgive me for my poor leadership over the previous weeks.

I will never forget the shocked looks on team members faces and the long minute of complete silence until the tension in the air was relieved by one brave soul saying "It hasn't all been bad!"

I went on to explain that this was a valuable lesson for me. Barry did me a big favor by making me aware of my behavior. He gave me an opportunity to do something about it.

From that day forward I promised myself that I would always do my best to be positive, to inspire and encourage others.

This meant rethinking and rephrasing the words that had been coming out of my mouth. When I was tempted to say, "The staff are not doing their jobs" instead I would say, "let's look at areas where we can make improvements". When I saw certain things being neglected, I encouraged my staff to speak up and let me know when repairs or better equipment was needed. It also meant encouraging an environment where all team members could acknowledge what was going on, give each other feedback and help each other by sharing teachable moments. We can always learn from each other.

When we learn to acknowledge mistakes or inappropriate behavior and then choose to do something about it, the outcome is usually positive. It also shows others that you are human and not perfect.

A quote by a famous football coach is a good reminder about taking personal responsibility when it comes to acknowledgement.

*"The superior man blames himself
and the inferior man blames others"*
—Coach Don Shula

 **Advice**

"Acknowledge Feedback"

- **Listen carefully** to the feedback you are receiving.

- **Stay calm** and avoid an immediate reaction.

- **Pause and take a deep breath** so you can respond rather than react.

- **Be sure to ask questions and paraphrase** what you hear so you really understand what has been said.

- **Accept the feedback with an open mind,** keep your voice calm and refrain from counter attacking, making excuses or arguing. You are in control of what you do with the information. Consider what is valid, what you can learn, what will help you grow and change for the better.

- **Thank the person** for bringing it to your attention.

- **Show your appreciation** for the feedback by doing something about it.

Take Action!

How will you acknowledge feedback?

- Are you using mistakes as opportunities to learn or finding fault to discipline someone?
- Do you believe that feedback from peers is just as important as the feedback from management?
- Are you encouraging team members to do self and peer evaluations?
- Do you encourage those you supervise to evaluate you?

Story 2 - ACKNOWLEDGE

Your Work is Important!

Troy was tall, dark haired and a very social individual. He started work at our recreation center as a volunteer at age 12. After acquiring qualifications for instructing and lifeguarding, he worked for several years on a part-time basis while attending school. After his grade 12 graduation he was in a quandary, not knowing what he should do to further his education. He chose to work as many hours as he could because he loved his work and the people he worked with.

One day, I remember starting a conversation with him about his future plans.

"What are your plans for the future, now that you have graduated from high school and are onto a new journey in your life?" After a long pause, his reply surprised me.

"Well, I am just a lifeguard. I don't have a clue what I should do in the future"

"Have you ever considered why your work here is important? Have you ever given some thought to all the skills you have learned on the job?"

"Well, no, not really, I haven't given much thought to either."

For the next hour we talked about why Troy's work was important and about all the skills he had learned on the job that would be helpful to him in other positions. He knew that he was keeping people safe while using the facility. He knew that he was able to teach people the important life skill of swimming. He could see he was encouraging them to have fun.

What he didn't think about was how he was keeping people active and healthy. How he was helping seniors with their mobility. How he was ultimately improving the health and happiness of thousands of people who use the facility. How he was helping to keep people out of hospitals thus creating less strain on the healthcare system.

After some reflection, he was able to rattle off the skills he had learned on the job, skills that helped build his confidence and skills that would serve him well in other positions in the future.

The list included:

- Experience as a teacher
- Preparing lesson plans
- Speaking in front of others
- Experience in customer service and public relations with people of all ages
- Dealing with challenging people situations: scared kids, unruly patrons, rule breakers and those with special needs
- Experience problem solving
- Dealing with emergency situations and providing first aid
- Learning great administration skills such as how to organize, keep inventories and set up schedules
- experience being a team player
- learning about collaboration
- experience as a supervisor
- practising negotiation skills
- providing orientation and training
- keeping an environment safe, healthy and clean
- how to have fun

"I guess I have learned a lot," Troy admitted.

"What careers would you be able to pursue as a result of this experience?"

"I could further my education in many fields. I could teach, I could train in the medical field or in emergency services. I could coach. Be a social worker. Work in health and safety or in customer service or be a public relations person."

"Troy, I want you to remember that all the things you have experienced so far in your life will lead to your next journey. It is really important to seriously think about what interests you the most and what work you would be most happy doing."

After I talked with Troy, I could see his motivation and pride in his job increased. Over time, he went on to pursue a rewarding career as a manager in recreation. He made me realize how important it is to remind others of the importance of their work.

 **Advice**

"Acknowledge Why Work is Important"

- **Help them realize how they make a difference** in the lives of their customers. For example: Our team teaches important life skills, helps to keep patrons healthy, fit and flexible, away from the doctor's office and the hospital. Our work is ultimately helping to reduce the strain on our health care system.

- **Challenge them to make the experience fun for all** and do things like keeping track of the number of times they can make a customer laugh or chronic complainers smile.

- **Help them figure out ways to gauge day-to-day success** by reducing the time it takes to serve a customer or make the line-ups move more quickly.

- **Team members need to feel that their supervisor knows and cares** about them beyond their job.

- **They also need to know that by doing their jobs well they make customers happy.** When people are happy other things in their lives go better and they are more likely to have a good day, good week and good month, etc.

- **Supporting team members' development** is crucial. Acknowledging what they have a passion for and helping them to learn and grow in their positions. This means helping to prepare them for other work opportunities they may pursue later.

- **I believe as supervisors, we have an obligation to society to help employees learn** so we pass on team members who are better educated than when they first came to us.

- **Most important action is to catch people doing things right** and reinforce their good work.

Take Action!

How will you acknowledge why work is important?

- Do you have any staff that think they are "just a _____" who you can re-energize by telling them the importance of their work?
- What feedback do you provide to team members that reinforces why their work is important?
- How do you help team members realize what they do does contribute to making a difference in people's lives?
- How are you encouraging the growth and development of each team member and building on their strengths?

Chapter Four

ROLE MODEL

"Leadership is not something you do to people. It's something you do with people."
—Ken Blanchard, Management Expert and Author of *The One Minute Manager*

The Rec Coach's Heads Up on being a great role model
ROLE MODEL is a learning process
ROLE MODEL the right things

Story 1 - ROLE MODEL

Paying Attention Pays Off!

Since the age of 12 when I started working as a volunteer for the summer, I have always observed and paid attention to the teachers and leaders around me, watching how they interact and treat people. Little did I know at the time I was preparing and learning for my leadership roles in the future.

When I was still in these young, formative years I remember a number of these leaders. There was Bev, an attractive, young woman who always seemed to be happy and upbeat no matter what happened. That was before she was promoted. After she was promoted to be the new supervisor, however, I couldn't believe she was the same person. She acted very differently. She was condescending and thought she knew what was best for everyone. She barked orders, bossed us around and was always quick to tell us what we were doing wrong. She seldom thanked us for what we were able to accomplish and she always reminded us of who was boss.

A couple of years later I recall Supervisor Steve, very fit, and a really nice guy, but not the greatest communicator. His expectations were never clear. That summer, the team always seemed to be in chaos. We spent most of our time being reactive instead of proactive because there was no planning being done. As a result, we were always having staff dilemmas, fixing scheduling mistakes, dealing with disappointed customers and the days seemed endless.

Then there was Dorothy, she was a little older than other supervisors, but what a great communicator, always giving clear instructions and checking in on how everyone was doing. She insisted on having regular meetings with everyone's participation. She encouraged feedback and sharing of ideas. She really wanted people to do what they were good at, but also expected everyone to work hard and do their fair share. The remarkable thing about Dorothy was she wanted people to enjoy their work. She was enthusiastic, inspiring and always made everyone feel special.

When I turned 18, the Recreation Director at the time had confidence in my abilities, insisting that I could take on the role of Supervisor. I didn't have any formal training and I could certainly have used more guidance. I remembered the summers with Bev, Steve and Dorothy and gave a lot of thought to their leadership styles.

While in the bookstore at University, my eyes were drawn to a book called, "The One Minute Manager" by author Ken Blanchard. As I read one of the quotes on the outside cover, I was reminded of Supervisor Bev:

"When was the last time someone caught you doing something right?"

Flipping through the book, I liked the fact that it was an easy read and only 112 pages. I purchased the book and that very night read it from cover to cover, relating to many aspects. I also realized that if I wanted to become a great leader I needed to learn as much as I could from other great leaders.

Author Ken Blanchard became one of my best book friends. One book led to another, then as many other authors and experts entered my life, I worked hard trying to put what I was learning into action.

Along this journey, I learned about a supervisor's disease called Supervisoritis. Now, when I have the opportunity to coach new supervisors I remind them to stay away from this disease and be cautious of the symptoms that start when your head swells because you have a new title. Examples are when you think it's great to be able to tell people what to do and when you think you don't have to do what you expect others to do because you are the boss.

Supervisor Bev was a perfect example of having Supervisoritis. I remember her barking orders. The performance feedback she would give us was all negative, bringing up things from months ago that were never discussed at the time they actually happened.

As a young supervisor in a position to help others, I soon realized that the leadership books I had been reading helped me to learn that I could rely on my team members to solve problems, come up with solutions and put things in to action.

Being mindful of the importance of developing leaders, I included team members in decision making. I wanted them to have as many experiences as possible. On many occasions I was pleasantly surprised with their logical solutions.

I learned that team members who were supported and encouraged rarely let you down. When someone tried their best and something went wrong, the encouragement they got from others was critical for them to try again. Team members knew it was okay to make a mistake as long as they learned from it and didn't make the same mistake again.

I learned the more you let team members know how much you value what they do, the more they will contribute. I believe that there is no better feeling than to know you are making a difference and that others appreciate your efforts.

 **Advice**

"Role Model"
Don't make these top 10 Mistakes that Managers often make:

1. Not asking for feedback or ideas or suggestions from their staff
2. Supervising everyone in the same way
3. Playing favorites
4. Keeping all the interesting work for themselves
5. Delegating without clear expectations
6. Reprimanding team members in front of others
7. Distancing themselves from those they supervise
8. Not supporting the team
9. Not training and developing team members
10. Taking credit for something others have done

Take Action!

How will you take action to be a great role model?

- What have you learned from others that you want to model?
- What have you learned from others that you don't want to model?
- Which of the top 10 mistakes are you making? How could you adjust your approach to avoid these mistakes?

Story 2 - ROLE MODEL

Role Model the Right Things!

When David, the new Recreation Director, was hired, I was very optimistic that he was our new leader. I prepared my team by speaking positively about the change and providing them with information on his background and experience. I introduced and invited him to participate in our monthly meetings. I wanted him to get to know the individuals who led our large team ensuring that the recreation facilities in our town were programmed, operated and maintained effectively.

Within a few weeks, I was disappointed to witness many things that I believed should not be done by a highly educated individual who was a role model. He was disorganized and for many meetings he arrived late, rushing in with a jumble of papers and was rarely prepared to discuss the items on the agenda. He often made promises about doing things and then did not follow through on them.

David also made a habit of checking his BlackBerry during meetings, and on more than one occasion took phone calls and left the room while the rest of us waited patiently for him to speak to certain items on the agenda. It was obvious whoever called was much more important than we were. His lack of manners and respect for our time was quite evident.

It was very disconcerting to discover that David's leadership style was not congruent with what he had described in the job interview. As a member of the interview panel I had asked:

"David, when you started your last position, describe how you approached your first year with the team you supervised."

"I took the time to get to know team members, to see how things were going before I suggested any changes," was how he answered my question.

David clearly was not walking the talk. In my first meeting with him, he questioned everything I was doing and made a comment that made me feel disrespected and unheard. He said:

"Where I used to work, we didn't do things that way. You may want to re-evaluate. You need to make changes."

It was in that moment, I felt that my years of experience, the positive feedback from all my former supervisors and the reputation for my ability to lead a very strong and effective team was not at all considered. It was the first time in my career that I did not feel valued.

Over the next couple of months I felt very anxious, under pressure and always had a lump in my stomach when I received emails and voice messages from him. I was not inspired to want to meet with him, nor share what I was doing. I believed that anything I said would be challenged. Eventually, his micro managing style made me feel very inadequate. Many times I was ready to quit!

It was a difficult time for everyone on the team he supervised. David was quick to make changes; would frequently do things like change meeting dates or times and then be frustrated with us when team members were not all in attendance. The team's history as avid planners and our preference to be proactive rather than reactive was losing its effectiveness.

Had David been true to the words spoken in his interview, taken time to get to know team members and learn how things were being done, it would have saved all of us so much grief, disruption and anxiety. Instead, many of the changes he insisted upon had to be reversed later.

I soon decided that I was not going to allow this person to drive me away. I knew that I had to do something to change all this. The next opportunity I had to meet one-on-one with David, I decided to discuss my feelings and frustrations.

When David sat down in my office, I was shaking inside and my heart was racing. I told him that I needed to say something that was difficult for me to share because I don't like confrontation.

"David, I feel very frustrated because you haven't really taken the time to get to know me or my team members. You are always suggesting that we make changes before you really understand how we are currently operating. I am disappointed at some of the things I have observed you doing. They go against what I believe demonstrates being a great role model."

I paused, took a deep breath and then said, "Would you be open to my feedback?"

David looked surprised and then said, "Please tell me more".

I told David that I had written a list of expectations of those that I supervise. I handed him a copy as I continued to explain.

"These are the skills that I believe make a big difference in being effective in a leadership role. I want you to know that over the years I have made a lot of mistakes. I have always worked hard to learn better ways of leading people. I work hard to be the best role model I can be. "

David stared long and hard at the sheet of paper I had given him. I worried that he might take it all the wrong way. After a long and tense several minutes he said:

"I appreciate your candid feedback. I am sorry to have disappointed you."

The meeting continued with me sharing some specific examples of my disappointments.

"Remember the time recently when you and I and three colleagues were meeting to make some decisions on a project we were all involved in. Ten minutes into the meeting, you and Susan both got calls on your BlackBerries. You both left the room for 15 and 20 minutes leaving the three of us to continue discussions. When you both returned, we had to start all over. How do you think it made us feel?"

David turned red in the face and swallowed hard and said:

"I do remember the meeting. What was I thinking?"

We continued to talk for more than an hour about how things could be different and we agreed to meet again in a couple of days to continue our discussion.

As I drove home that night, I was surprised and very relieved at how David had taken my comments. It seemed that he was open to my feedback and willing to make some changes.

It took several meetings to start to feel like progress was being made. David had a chance to explain that the reason he questioned everything was not to micro manage, but to learn how I did things. This was a good lesson for me about different perceptions. I believe it is difficult to make a judgment unless you observe something first hand. I would have felt more support from the beginning if he had taken some time to be present and on occasion spent more time around the team.

Over the next weeks and months there were many perceptions to clarify. Progress was made and we eventually worked well together. Because I had opened up and we were able to have some frank discussions, we both learned.

I truly believe that everything that happens in our lives happens for a reason. When I was in this situation, I pondered for several days what the reason might be. What was I supposed to learn from this experience? Well, I learned about perceptions. I learned how strong my beliefs are about role modeling the right things. I learned that I could help him be a better role model. I also realized that there was much I could learn from him too.

"A leader is one who knows the way,
goes the way, and shows the way."
—John Maxwell, Author and Speaker

"Role Model the Right Things"

Our job as Supervisors and Managers, is to inspire the people around us to do great work.

Lead by example:
- Show a positive example, acting with integrity and sincerity at all times.
- Show them how to do their best.
- Do what you say you will do.
- Do the right thing, at the right time and for the right reason.
- Come prepared if you want team members to be prepared.

Have a clear set of Values:
- Spend some time determining a clear set of personal values.
- Build common values among the team that help to guide behavior and decision making.
- Clarify what is really important and how work time should be spent.

Focus on being in the present with one another:
- Prevent distractions so there are no interruptions.
- Be respectful of other people's time.

Take Action!
Consider how you role model the right things.
- What do you need to do to improve as a role model?
- When in a new position, how will you get off on the right foot?
- What are your team values?

Chapter Five

TRUST

"**Trust** is the essence of Leadership"
—General Colin Powell, U.S.
Statesman

The Rec Coach's Heads Up on Trust
TRUSTing your team is critical
TRUST over Micro-Managing

Story 1 - TRUST

Trust is Critical!

As a young supervisor, I learned the way some manager's operate is "no news" is good news. I would only hear when I was doing something that he didn't approve of. It was always a surprise when he brought this to my attention because his expectations were never really clear. I was doing the best I could with what I knew at the time. Oprah often says, "When you know better, you do better."

In one of my positions, I was hired in an assistant director's role and when I started work I was to be trained by the woman who was taking maternity leave. As it turned out, she struggled with severe nausea and was only able to spend a few hours with me.

Ron, the director was on vacation at the time so I was left to fend for myself. Before I took the position I had heard from some very good sources that Ron would be a good guy to work for. He had a reputation of being organized and running a very efficient operation.

I realized right away that everything was so well documented and organized with the systems and procedures in place that I could practically teach myself what was expected in the position. An employee orientation manual provided all the answers to any questions I had regarding everything from the organizational structure to what I needed to know about emergency procedures. There were checklists to guide staff in keeping everything running smoothly and good historical information for reference that was beneficial to plan for the future.

After two weeks, Ron contacted me to see how things were going and when I reassured him that things were going really well, he decided to take another two weeks of vacation. My confidence immediately soared with the thought that Ron believed that things would go well in his absence. I remember feeling so trusted!

When he returned from his vacation, I had settled in, loved my new position and noted questions that I wanted more information about.

Several months went by and my mom asked me how my new job was going to which I replied:

"I think things are going really well but I don't know for sure."

"Why don't you ask Ron how you are doing?"

Ask...I thought....what a concept? In my mind, I was thinking that he should be telling me how I am doing.

"When in doubt, why wouldn't you ask?"

When I did ask for feedback, Ron said,

"Well, I think things are going really well. I didn't worry about anything when I was away. So far so good. I am glad I hired you."

That made me feel better although I was interested in knowing specifically what he thought was going really well. Instead, I was left wondering, was everything really going well? At the time Ron told me he appreciated me asking, as it was a good reminder to him that we all need feedback. I didn't dare ask any further questions right then for fear of him bringing up something that I didn't want to hear.

After years of experience if I had the chance to do it over, I would have asked for more specific feedback. Every opportunity I have now, I encourage people to ask for feedback. We all know that it doesn't feel right to work in a situation where you don't know how you are doing.

Author Ken Blanchard says: "Feedback is the Breakfast of Champions!"

Why wait for feedback to come to us?

People learn valuable lessons from feedback, from problems that need to be solved, from difficult experiences and in the process they learn about trust and building trust.

"The best way to find out if you can **trust** somebody is to **trust** them."

—Ernest Hemingway, Author and Journalist

OACH Advice

"Building Trust"

Being able to trust comes from sharing feedback and supporting one another. When trust is present, individuals and teams are more confident, committed and energized. They deal better with change and end up being more productive. Trust is fragile and can easily be broken.

Trust is broken by what people do to each other including blame, gossip, twisting the truth, withholding information, taking credit for other's work.

Strong working relationships are built on trust. Team members need to be able to trust their leaders to make the best decisions for the organization and leaders need to be able to trust the abilities of their team members. When you have a strong foundation of trust your employees know what is expected of them and what they can expect from you.

Tools for building trust:
- Be a great role model - lead by example
- Keep promises

- Communicate openly and honestly in a respectful way
- Ask for feedback
- Get to know each other personally and see your team members as people
- Never place blame
- Put your heads together to solve problems and ensure they don't happen again
- Set up a team charter that clarifies values, purpose and roles

Take Action!
How are you trusting your team?

- What are you doing or not doing to show that you trust others?
- Are there times when you haven't kept your promises?
- Are there situations right now that need an open and honest discussion?
- When was the last time you asked for feedback?

Story 2 - TRUST

Trust or Micro Manage?

A good leader does not micro manage others unless individuals demonstrate that they want to be supervised closely and guided on every step. My experience with micro managers has led me to believe that these individuals lack the ability to trust others due to their own insecurities.

I have learned from other experts and from my own experience that if you treat people as if they are capable and smart, and allow them to do their work, they won't let you down. Team members who are allowed to be involved in helping to make decisions respond much better than those who aren't. Involving team members builds trust. Good leaders take every opportunity they can to build trust.

After a large renovation of our aquatics facility, it was time to determine how the staff would keep the patrons safe in this new environment. Who better to decide, than the lifeguards who would be responsible. So at one of our team meetings, I asked them.

"How would you like to be the creators of procedures for our lifeguarding stations, rotations and the new guidelines for our swimmers?" As I looked around the room, John smiled right away and said, "I would like to help."

Carol joined in too. "Yup I'm in."

Tim added his approval. "Wow, really? That means we will want to play on the new slides to figure things out!"

"Cool." Cheryl confirmed the group's excitement and readiness.

"We can do this!"

After hearing that these experienced lifeguards were all keen and up for the challenge, I gave them a couple of instructions.

"Whatever you come up with, I know will be logical and easily justified. Keep in mind that safety is our top priority, while at the same time; we want people to have fun. Your team will want to be comfortable reinforcing all guidelines when educating the public."

In no time, the team created an effective system for the lifeguarding stations and rotations that included different scenarios for only a few swimmers to a capacity of 650 swimmers. They also created strategies for communication with hand signals for relaying messages to other lifeguards.

The safety orientation that was given to all schools and rental groups was also updated. Decisions were made about the allocation of pool spaces that encouraged flexibility and the accommodation of patrons needs.

When determining guidelines, the team had remembered previous discussions about having a good explanation of why guidelines are needed and how to write them. Guidelines should be a short list, phrased in a positive way, and include only the necessary guidelines. After spending time experimenting on the new slides and toys, they were able to determine what would help to keep patrons safe.

After the renovation and preparation to open to the public, there were new processes and procedures to put in place for the Customer Service Representatives too. I put them to the task as well. This team created guidelines for providing customer service ensuring patrons would receive consistent, great service from all team members.

These included answering the telephone, handling patron concerns, cash procedures, security, daily routine procedures and work lists.

These front line workers have a wealth of information and can assist in making improvements, especially in the areas of their day-to-day work. It is important for them to have training and the empowerment to solve a customer's dilemma on the spot and not have to wait for a supervisor's permission.

How many times have you waited at a counter for someone else to "authorize or approve something" because the team member serving you didn't have the authority? This is another example of ways employees are micro managed and often made to feel inadequate. If front line staff were trusted, imagine the time saved for the customer, the staff person and the leaders of the organization.

 OACH **4 Tips on Trust**

When Feeling Micro Managed

1. Be sure to discuss the situation with this person and share your perceptions and feelings.

    EXAMPLE: "I noticed that you've been checking in with me about this task a lot. It makes me think or worries me that you don't trust me. Can we talk about how to make this work better for both of us?

2. When tasks are delegated to you, be sure that you are clear on the outcomes expected.

    EXAMPLE: "So, the critical outcomes you are expecting include first having a draft of procedures prepared for feedback and discussion at our next team meeting?"

3. Be sure to keep your manager informed so they don't feel the need to check up on you.

    EXAMPLE: "I will keep you in the loop and provide you with a project update at our biweekly meetings. If I encounter any difficulties with the timelines, I will let you know right away."

4. Be sure to let the person know that you are willing to work on building a trusting relationship and when in doubt, you will ask questions and seek guidance to ensure you accomplish the outcome that has been agreed upon.

    EXAMPLE: " I will be sure to ask you questions that I have as the new program is developed. I have lots of ideas that I want to discuss with you when it comes time to implement and I will appreciate your guidance."

Building trust takes time and comes from continuous day-to-day actions that demonstrate your willingness to do your best, help others, be honest, admit mistakes, to listen, show interest, and do what you say you will do.

Take Action!
How are you building trust?

- How will you get input from team members when there are decisions to be made?
- What policies are in place that prevent front line team members from solving problems on the spot?
- What could be changed so team members don't have to "check with their supervisors"?
- What steps do you need to take to build more trusting relationships?

CONCLUSION

I am leaving you with 5 keys to Leading with HEART that can make a big difference in developing and leading teams that care.

Leaders with heart are continually aware of how they are interacting with others and they are consciously aware of helping others become leaders too.

If you implement these 5 keys, your job will be easier and much more rewarding. Those you lead will know you care because they have the support and encouragement to help them gain confidence as they grow and develop as leaders. Remember your role is to develop leaders for the future. The strength of the team depends on the strength of the leadership.

"If your actions inspire others to dream more, learn more, do more and become more, you are a leader."
—John Quincey Adams, 6th President USA

Great leaders lead with HEART.

Helping

Encouraging

Acknowledging

Role modeling

Trusting team members

5 Keys to Leading with HEART

Heart Key 1

Help team members get a good start by offering an effective orientation to the position and the organization.

Leader Actions: Have a detailed plan including who does what, when, where, how and why.

Make sure team members are clear on what is expected of them.

Heart Key 2

Encourage team members to ask questions, connect with others, share information and get to know others.

Leader Actions: Reinforce getting to the root of a problem, good listening, sharing ideas, opinions and experiences .

Heart Key 3

Acknowledge the importance of everyone's work and the importance of receiving feedback.

Leader Actions: Share how work makes a difference to the organization and the customers they serve.

Receive feedback with an open mind and then choose to do things differently.

Use mistakes as opportunities to learn.

Involve team members in evaluating each other.

Heart Key 4

Role Model as you learn from other great role models.

Leader Actions: Walk the Talk and Walk the Walk consistently. Become someone others like to follow because of your vision, inspiration and positive attitude.

Have a good discussion about team values and perceptions.

Heart Key 5

Trust team members and prevent them from being micro managed.

Leader Actions: Let team members know exactly what is expected of them.

Focus on roles, outcomes, best results and then empower them to get things done.

Keep this key wisdom in mind as you lead with HEART.

Every day of the week make a conscious effort to be helpful, encouraging, acknowledging, be a great role model while trusting your team to succeed.

And remember...

"Lead with your HEART and your team will never let you down!"

Thank you for reading! I hope these simple stories, the Rec Coaches advice, and all the questions to reflect on how well you are doing, inspire you to continue to learn and grow as a leader.

Good Luck with your leadership journey and remember to put your heart into it!

I would love to hear your leadership stories and get your feedback, especially if you are in the recreational services community.

Please visit www.thereccoach.com to share your comments.

The Rec Coach can assist you in developing the leaders on your team.
To contact Edith Martin:
Email: edith@thereccoach.com
www.thereccoach.com

THE REC COACH'S SUGGESTED READING LIST

It was difficult to choose which books to list here as hundreds of books have influenced my leadership development. I believe the important thing is to continue to learn from others and make your development a life long journey of self-improvement.

The Rec Coach's Lead with Your Head:
Building Smart Teams
by Edith Martin

This book focuses on Teamwork and shares 5 important keys for creating a positive working environment for team members.

The Rec Coach's Lead with Your Hands:
Creating Award-Winning Service Teams
by Edith Martin

This book focuses on Customer Service and shares 5 important keys for a leader wanting to create a team with a genuine focus on providing award winning service.

The One-Minute Manager
by Ken Blanchard and Spencer Johnson

This was the first of many Ken Blanchard books that influenced my leadership journey. It shares three very practical management techniques. The book is brief, simple and provides information that works!

The 7 Habits of Highly Effective People
by Stephen R. Covey

This is a book of powerful lessons in personal change. Since reading this book many years ago, I have continually used the concepts shared.

Great Leaders Grow- Becoming a Leader for Life
by Ken Blanchard and Mark Miller

A great read emphasizing that our capacity to grow determines our capacity to lead and shares how Leaders grow leaders by focusing on certain areas to remain effective throughout their lives.

The Leader in You
by Dale Carnegie

A classic and timeless read on how to win friends and influence people and succeed in a changing world.

The Five Dysfunctions of a CEO
by Patrick Lencioni

A wonderful story that shares powerful lessons that are barriers to successful leadership.

Developing the Leader Within You
by John C Maxwell

A great book that teaches how to find people with potential, develop them into leaders and then turn them into a team. He shares practical real-life examples that inspire you to take action.

The Truth about Managing People
by Stephen P Robbins

A collection of management research that is shared in 63 "Truths" offering real solutions for the make-or-break problems faced by every manager.

Help Them Grow or Watch Them Go
by Beverly Kaye & Julie Winkle Giulioni

A great book of practical tips, guidelines and templates for employee career development which is the single most powerful tool managers have for driving retention, engagement, productivity and results.

ABOUT THE AUTHOR

Edith Martin was born and raised in small town Alberta, Canada, and was an active child in sports and music. She pursued a degree in Education with a major in Physical Education, later acquiring a Human Resources Management Certificate while building a long career in Recreation.

With 40 years in Recreation Facility Management and her experience leading a variety of teams, Edith Martin "The Rec Coach" shares lessons from personal experiences that have made a difference in developing and leading teams.

A former school teacher and sports coach, Edith is also a Past President and Honorary Life Member of the Alberta Association of Recreation Facility Personnel.

As a seasoned facilitator in leadership and customer service training, team building and strategic planning, Edith continues to provide practical wisdom to organizations and businesses.

Edith is a life long learner, a dedicated member of Rotary International and strongly believes in giving back to help others.

To contact Edith Martin:
Email: edith@thereccoach.com
www.thereccoach.com

Watch for the release of other books by
The Rec Coach, Edith Martin

Learn 5 "SMART" teamwork strategies for transforming your team.

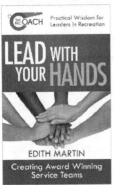

Learn 5 important customer service strategies to "SERVE" your customers better.

Taking Action
Your Notes on
"Helping"

_____

_____

_____

_____

_____

_____

_____

_____

_____

_____

Taking Action
Your Notes on
"Encouraging"

_____

_____

_____

_____

_____

_____

_____

_____

_____

_____

Taking Action
Your Notes on
"Acknowledging"

_____

_____

_____

_____

_____

_____

_____

_____

_____

_____

Taking Action
Your Notes on
"Role Modelling"

_____

_____

_____

_____

_____

_____

_____

_____

_____

_____

Taking Action
Your Notes on
"Trusting"

_____

_____

_____

_____

_____

_____

_____

_____

_____

_____